The Word of God in Our Hands

By Cushroo Bejon

WIPF & STOCK · Eugene, Oregon

Wipf and Stock Publishers
199 W 8th Ave, Suite 3
Eugene, OR 97401

The Word of God in Our Hands
By Bejon, Cushroo
Copyright©2018 Apostolos
ISBN 13: 978-1-5326-6883-8
Publication date 9/16/2018
Previously published by Apostolos, 2018

Author Preface

The writing of this short document arose out of an attempt to reconcile the teachings of Jesus with what I had been taught as a follower of the prophet Zoroaster. Jesus says, "I am the way and the truth and the life. No-one comes to the Father except through me" (John 14:6). These words of Jesus are diametrically opposed to what I was taught as a child. Different religious systems, I was told, were like climbing a mountain by differing paths, but you finished at the top whichever path you took. I needed to find out if the claim Jesus made was true, so I turned to the Bible to investigate. There are many religious teachers who stress the need to do good but fail to deal with the evil we do. I discovered that Jesus not only recognised this failing of humankind but dealt with the problem in His own unique way. He gave His own life to secure my forgiveness, and so I committed my life to Him—to follow His teachings as revealed in the Bible, the Word of God. Not only for these moral reasons for obeying His teaching but also in the pursuit of truth I have traced the evidence of antiquity that the Bible is the true Word of God.

I am pleased to acknowledge the help given to me in producing this booklet by my wife, Jane, in typing and that of my son, James, in IT support and advice.

Introduction

This booklet explains how despite human error, and attempted fraud, God has ensured that the truth of His Word has been preserved.

The first chapter examines the care with which the copyists of the Old Testament ensured we have an accurate account of the Word of God. Chapter 2 deals with how the increasing numbers of New Testament manuscripts were collated to provide strong evidence for the validity of the text as we have it. Many men voluntarily endangered and even sacrificed their lives to ensure that subsequent generations may have access to the Word of God. In chapter 3, the Dead Sea Scrolls section, whilst tracing the discovery of the scrolls, we deal with the dating of the scrolls and the evidence they provide to support the text of the Old Testament. Chapter 4, The English Bible traces the development of the English Bible and reinforces the integral connection between the two Testaments. The Old Testament in its entirety belongs to our Bible and is the foundation on which the New Testament is laid.

1. The Old Testament

"In the beginning, God created the heavens and the earth." (Genesis 1:1)

The Old Testament (OT) was written chiefly in Hebrew, but a few small sections were in Aramaic. These are found in Jeremiah 10:11, Daniel 2:4b–7:28, and Ezra 4:8–6:18; 7:12–26. Like Hebrew, Aramaic is a Semitic language. Both languages were used in early Biblical times, hence Laban and Jacob named the heap of stones differently: Laban in Aramaic, Jacob in Hebrew (Genesis 31:47). Both languages continued to be used in Israel throughout her existence, though only the officials tended to be conversant with Aramaic and Hebrew; the common people spoke only Hebrew (see 2 Kings 18:26). After Alexander the Great conquered Egypt, Greek settlers were introduced into Alexandria in Egypt, where a large number of Jews were already resident. They became very conversant with Greek which became their native language. To meet the needs of these Jews in Alexandria, the OT was translated into Greek. To start with, just the Pentateuch was translated, but later the remaining books of the OT were also translated. This translation of the OT from Hebrew to Greek was called the Septuagint because it was allegedly completed in just 70 days by 70 translators (72 in earlier accounts). The Septuagint circulated not only in Egypt, but also in Palestine and Asia. Work was started in the 3rd century BCE, but it took until 2 BCE to be completed and copied.

After returning from the captivity in Babylon, the Jews in Palestine began to adopt Aramaic as the language of everyday use. Since the Scriptures were written in Hebrew, paraphrases or targums were produced, probably for the benefit of common folk who were less familiar with ancient Hebrew (see Nehemiah 8:1–8). At the same time, the Talmudists (the scholars) explained and commented on the text, having brought together all the traditions, both textual and explanatory.

The last OT prophet, Malachi, completed his ministry in about 400 BCE soon after the rebuilding of the temple in Jerusalem, when Nehemiah was the governor. There followed a dark period of 400 years, during which time there was no prophet in Israel until John the Baptist appeared. During these same 400 years, Antiochus Epiphanes, the notorious Syrian King, defiled the Temple in Jerusalem and attempted to abolish the Jewish religion. Judas Maccabeus and his brothers led the nation to take up arms and eventually defeated Antiochus. A number of writings in Hebrew, Aramaic, and Greek (with translations in Latin, Syriac, Ethiopic, Arabic and Armenian) began to appear and were later known as the Apocrypha. There are 12 or 14 books, depending on how they are subdivided, which include the books of Esdras, Tobit, Judith, the additions to the Book of Esther, the Wisdom of Solomon, Ecclesiasticus, Baruch, the Letter of Jeremiah, the Prayer of Azariah, and the Song of the Three Young Men, Suzanna, Bel and the Dragon, the Prayer of Manasseh, the First Book of the Maccabees, and the Second Book of the Maccabees. The books can be categorised as historical, religious, fictional, ethical, or apocalyptic.

The preservation of the OT text became one of the chief concerns of the Jews after the fall of Jerusalem in 70 CE. At about this time, serious discussions were held amongst the Rabbis about which books of the sacred writings should be considered canonical and hence serve as a rule of faith. In addition to the 39 canonical books, there were 15 other books, which are part of a Jewish assortment of literature from the period 300 BCE to 100 CE. These apocryphal books (listed above) were not ultimately accepted in the Hebrew Canon by the Jews in Palestine or in Alexandria. Notable second century CE Rabbi Akiva was most outspoken against their inclusion in any Hebrew Canon (see James, 1924).

Despite early references to a Canon of Hebrew Scriptures (e.g. in Sirach), it was many years later that the earliest Hebrew Bible we can be certain of was produced. In about 700 CE, the Masoretes (whose headquarters were in Tiberias), established a final Hebrew text based on all the available evidence. They also set up rigorous rules to ensure that the text was accurately copied to replace old, damaged copies, needed for daily use in synagogues throughout Palestine and abroad. Such care was exercised with regard to the copying of the Scriptures that old or damaged copies were stored in a special cupboard in the synagogue, termed a genizah, prior to burial in consecrated ground. To ensure accuracy of copying, they numbered the letters, words and verses of every book, even the middle word of each book and the number of times each letter was used. Anything that could be counted seems to have been counted to ensure that even one "jot or tittle" was not accidentally omitted. They also added vowels to the Hebrew text via a system of dots and dashes (mostly above and below the letters). To write without vowels may sound unusual to us, but it is not too difficult to grasp. Consider the following sentence: "n th bgnnng Gd crtd th hvns nd th rth." Most Christians would be able to read this sentence quite easily. But those unfamiliar with the Bible might well struggle. Besides, what if a heretic claimed that the text should be read, "In the beginning, a God created the heavens and the earth?" As can be seen, then, the work of the Masoretes was vital. It recorded the vowels of the text, which could otherwise have been lost, and fixed in place its meaning. The Masoretes then noted in the margins the traditional remarks collected from previous

generations, termed the Masorah (that is, "tradition.")
Even if they thought the text was wrong, they only put
their proposed corrections in the margins. The lesser
Masorah (abbreviated commentary) is written in the
left-hand margin, whereas the greater Masorah (fuller
commentary) is put in the margins to the right and on
the top.

It has to be accepted that in the process of making
copies of manuscripts, errors of hand, eye and mind
can occur. The job of the textual critic is to recover the
original text of Scripture. This may tempt some to
question whether we can ever have the true text of
Scripture, but it cannot be too strongly emphasised that
no fundamental doctrine rests on a disputed reading.
We have so many manuscripts of the OT and so many
quotations from the Church Fathers (as well as
translations in Latin, Greek, Syriac and the Samaritan
Pentateuch) that we can confidently claim to be able to
recover the original text. This is part of the overseeing
hand of God to leave us an authentic and reliable
witness to Himself.

The last factor to consider in the recovery of the
original text is the witness of the Dead Sea Scrolls. This
wonderful and illuminating find in 1948, moved the
date of our earliest OT manuscripts from the 9th
century CE back to the 1st century BCE, a jump of
nearly a thousand years. This text would have been

almost identical to the Hebrew OT text that our Lord Jesus used when He was in Israel. What better authentication could one ask for? There will be a further detailed treatment of the Dead Sea Scrolls later.

Amongst the very famous manuscripts (MSS) and papyri going back to the early part of the 2nd century are the following: *Chester Beatty Papyri* (3rd century CE); *Codex Sinaiticus* (4th century CE); *Codex Alexandrinus* (5th century CE); *Codex Vaticanus* (4th century CE); *Codex Ephraemi* (5th century CE); and many others. Compared with classical writings, there is an unprecedented wealth of manuscript support for both the OT, and the New Testament (NT).

There had been two infamous attempts to forge Biblical manuscripts, the first by Simonides in the 1850s and the second by Shapira in 1880. Simonides claimed to have a copy of the Gospel of Matthew and other portions of the New Testament, written in the first century, including Codex Sinaiticus. Shapira had cut strips of vellum from an ordinary synagogue scroll and written the Ten Commandments, with alterations, in an ancient script and had even added an eleventh commandment. He then claimed this was from the Book of Deuteronomy. But these fraudulent claims were soon exposed. X-ray analysis revealed that there was already writing on the strips of the old synagogue rolls, which he sought to hide by scraping the original inked surface. It is a testimony to the vigorous way in which the original text of Scripture has been preserved that forgeries such as these can be so easily spotted and rejected.

2. The New Testament

"In the beginning was the Word, and the Word was with God, and the Word was God." (John 1:1)

The form of Greek prevalent during the days when the NT was written was Koine Greek. By the 1st century CE, Koine Greek, being a mixture of different forms of Greek, included also some words from other languages and was widespread throughout the Roman empire. But the mother tongues of Jesus and His disciples were Aramaic and Hebrew and the NT has a few sayings of Jesus, preserved in Aramaic, in the Greek NT (Mark 5:41; 7:34; 15:34; 14:36; Romans 8:15; Galatians 4:6; 1 Corinthians 16:22). The books of the NT were written between the years of 50 to 100 CE. To start with, MSS were written on papyrus, and were written using block letters (uncial MSS). But papyrus is a fragile material. It was soon replaced by vellum (animal skin), which could be cut up, and eventually enabled the roll type manuscript (scroll) to be replaced by a codex (book). Vellum was much more durable and easier to write on (especially since, over time, uncial writing was replaced by cursive, joined up, writing, which is more legible on vellum than on papyrus).There are presently more than 5,000 MSS in whole or in part of the NT, and the closest fragment, in time, of a papyrus is dated to be within 50 years of the completion of the NT. This is called P52 and is now housed in the John Rylands Library at

Manchester, while the Alexandrinus and Sinaiticus MSS are at the MSS division of the British Museum in London. The NT is complete in the Sinaiticus, and most of it is in the Alexandrinus, both MSS belonging to the 4th and 5th centuries CE. In addition, there are more than 8,000 copies of the Latin Vulgate in existence, continuous references to Scripture in the Church Fathers' writings, and more than 2,000 lectionaries, in which texts are recorded for the purpose of daily and weekly readings. One may be tempted to doubt whether the original text may ever be recovered, but such reasoning does not take account of two crucial factors. The first is that the hand of God which has preserved His Word to mankind through so many precarious situations would not fail us at the end. The second factor to be considered is the overwhelmingly large number of supporting MSS, over 15,000, which far exceed that for any other ancient document. Further, as Sir Frederic Kenyon has pointed out:

"No fundamental doctrine of the Christian faith rests on a disputed reading."

It was the advent of printing that acted as a spur to the production of a Greek NT. Until this time the main interest was to produce a Latin NT, this being the language of scholarly literature. But it was soon realised that since the NT was originally written in Greek, this would be the best facility that could be

13

given to scholars who would then produce translations in their own mother tongues. The first scholar of note to embrace this concept was Erasmus. Unfortunately, Erasmus had access to only six Greek MSS, of varying age and completeness. He interpolated between the MSS and when compiling the text of the book of Revelation, he had to improvise by translating from the Latin to supply the missing verses. This work was completed and in 1516 the first printed Greek NT came off the press. The next scholar to devote himself to the task of improving the Greek NT was Stephanus. He succeeded in obtaining at least 15 further Greek MSS but these were relatively recent cursive copies, having dates close to the publishing date of his Greek NT. This was completed in 1550. Thereafter, increasing numbers of scholars published both the MSS they could easily access and in parallel columns the readings of other recently discovered MSS. This not only made available to scholars an increasing number of alternative readings, but also sowed the seeds of literary criticism, providing scholars with a basis for classifying MSS according to their authenticity.

Soon after the Canon of the NT was agreed amongst the early churches, a number of apocryphal works began to appear. Amongst these that were better known were the Epistle of Barnabas (not the Barnabas of the NT), the Shepherd of Hermas, the Infancy Gospels, the Apocalypse of Peter, the Ebionite Gospel, the Gospel according to Thomas, the Secret Sayings of Jesus, the Gospel according to the Hebrews and others. These publications were produced with the motive of providing supplementary information not given in the Gospels about Jesus before He entered His public ministry. Some of the spurious writings supported heretical beliefs similar to those of the Gnostics referred to in the Letter to the Colossians. These apocryphal and other similar writings were soon recognised by the early churches and their leaders as not having the authority of Scripture to act as a rule of faith and living.

That every effort is made to get as close as possible to the original text is vital. When the translator starts work, he needs to be sure about what the text says. The original documents composed by the NT authors (probably papyri) have perished by now. And copyists, sometimes working under even life-threatening conditions, could not ensure scrupulous accuracy. The task of the textual critic is, therefore, to sift through every available source, detecting errors in the copies and recovering the original text. To achieve this, he must first carefully study and assess the MSS available to him, which can be done in various ways. He must give due consideration to whether the MS is uncial or cursive, papyrus or vellum, also taking into account the age of the MS. Older MSS which were undiscovered for many years (e.g., the Codex Sinaiticus) are not likely to have been altered by copyists' errors; and uncial MSS were copied much earlier in time than cursive MSS and were produced in smaller numbers under carefully controlled conditions. By contrast, cursive MSS were copied in rapid succession, so copyists' mistakes were more frequent. The textual critic must also engage in textual analysis, which requires him to group MSS into different categories.

One way to group MSS together is on the basis of peculiarities of spelling or the use of certain words known as "variant readings." In this exercise the evidence of the Church Fathers' citations is also considered. Consideration is also given as to whether a manuscript is written on parchment or vellum. First an attempt is made to place MSS in groups and then, if possible, into larger groups known as archetypes. The identification of mistakes also becomes possible. One of the more common mistakes of copyists was, when faced with two MSS with slightly different wording, to include both words, which is known as conflation. (It was better, the copyist reasoned, to include an extra word than to risk losing some of the Word of God.) If one MS has the words "praising God" and the other "blessing God," the conflate reading would appear as "praising and blessing God." Such peculiar features help us to group MSS together, to trace their common ancestors, and to form archetypes. In general, three main archetype groups are recognised by most scholars (though there is not complete agreement amongst scholars as to these groupings or even the necessity to make groupings and to use this as a basis to accept or reject readings):

1. *Texts originating in Alexandria, including some papyri dated 200 CE, Codex B, citations of Origen and Codex Sinaiticus amongst others.*

2. *The 'Western' type text (so called because of its connection with countries such as France and Italy), which is supported by a number of papyri and in part by a few uncial MSS.*

3. *The Byzantine type, which is well supported numerically and is considered to be a revision carried out in Antioch in the 4th century.*

When it came to translating the Authorised Version in 1611, the underlying Greek and Hebrew texts needed to be established. The text compiled for the purpose of the AV translation came to be known as the Received Text. The OT text at this time was well established by the Masoretes, but, in the case of the NT, there were only six MSS available to Erasmus in Basel when he published his Greek NT, all of them 12th century or later, only one non-Byzantine and none of them complete. Stephanus used a further 15 MSS to produce his Greek NT in 1550, but most of the MSS he used were also comparatively late, that is, closer to the date of this compilation and therefore further removed from the original MSS. This combination of OT text and NT text became the Received Text from which the Authorised Version was translated.

Modern Bible scholars and translators have the advantage of access to many more fragments of manuscripts and even complete manuscripts of certain NT books, most of which come from a time much closer to the original writing of the NT (mostly 2nd and 3rd centuries CE). Even so, despite many differences between these and the earlier AV, it must again be stated that no significant discrepancies can be seen which would undermine any of the fundamental doctrines of Christianity.

3. The Dead Sea Scrolls

"He reveals deep and hidden things; He knows what lies in darkness, and light dwells with Him." (Daniel 2:22)

The discovery of the Dead Sea Scrolls is one of the miracles of the 20th century. Even Sir Frederic Kenyon, who worked for many years in the early 20th century as the director of the Manuscript Department of the British Museum, did not expect such early MSS to be discovered. Kenyon had studied ancient Biblical MSS covering the period from the 10th century onwards, in Greek, Hebrew, Latin and the translations in other languages.

The story of the finding of these scrolls is told in slightly differing forms. Here, I rely primarily on the account given by Dr. Millar Burrows (see Bibliography) because he was present at the time of the discovery. As the director of the American School of Oriental Research at Jerusalem, Burrows was very involved in assessing the authenticity and age of the scrolls. One account of the story is that a goatherd, having lost a goat, cast a stone at a hole in the cliff face at Khirbet Qumran on the North West edge of the Dead Sea. To his amazement he heard a sound of breaking pottery and thought he may have struck treasure. With the help of another goatherd, he entered the cave and found a number of pottery jars and broken pottery (potsherds). In the jars were leather scrolls, wrapped in linen and sealed in the jars with black pitch. The goatherds got the scrolls out, divided them among themselves, and went home not knowing what they had found. The following Saturday they brought the scrolls to the market in Bethlehem but could not find a buyer. The scrolls were brittle, and one was partially decomposed along one end, and because they were not written in Arabic, most of the people in Bethlehem could not understand their contents. They were taken to the Syrian Orthodox Monastery of St. Mark (in Jerusalem) on the supposition that they were Syriac, and word soon got around that these scrolls were for sale. Archbishop Samuel was brought one of the MSS and realised that the writing was Hebrew. At the same time, Professor Sukenik of the Hebrew University in Jerusalem also heard of the MSS being for sale. To cut a long story short, Archbishop Samuel acquired the following four MSS: 1. The Hebrew MSS of the Book of Isaiah (complete); 2. The first two chapters of the Book of Habakkuk with commentary (in Hebrew); 3. The Rule of the Community, for a religious Jewish community (probably Essenes); 4. The Lamech Scroll, written in Aramaic.

Meanwhile, Professor Sukenik purchased: 1. The War of the Sons of Light with the Sons of Darkness in Hebrew; 2. The Thanksgiving Psalms, also in Hebrew; 3. An incomplete manuscript of Isaiah. The first 37 chapters had deteriorated so that some of the writing had become illegible, but some recovery was later achieved by infra-red photography.

Eventually the MSS that were with Archbishop Samuel were loaned to the American School of Oriental Research. The MSS were photographed and sent to a number of Biblical scholars in America, England and Israel. In addition to these finds, roughly 40,000 fragments of MSS from the caves of Qumran were subsequently found and of these roughly 100 were from the books of the Bible and every OT book was included in these fragments except Esther. Here it may be thought at first that since we are dealing with just fragments crucial evidence may be missing, but it needs to be remembered that the Bible is so minutely scrutinised, especially by critics, that if any word or statement were different it would be seized upon immediately. The fragments included those from books of the Bible written in Greek (Septuagint), Aramaic, and Hebrew. Among the finds were also copper/bronze scrolls but these were not Biblical. All these fragments were cleaned and sorted, even using infra-red photography to make faded writing visible, and the work was done over a number of years by an international team of scholars. It is not likely that such evidence could really be fabricated to provide corroborative evidence for the extant MSS of the Bible, spanning a period of around a thousand years. The consensus based on Hebrew palaeography (the study of ancient writing) was that the complete Isaiah scroll has been dated to be between 175 and 150 BCE, whereas the partially damaged scroll was given a date between 1 to 25 CE. To me it is amazing to think that our Lord Jesus may well have used a text of the OT which was almost identical to the complete Isaiah scroll. Later, we will look in some detail at the differences between this Isaiah text and the Masoretic text as we have it now.

The dating of the scrolls is a skilled discipline. It is determined by the study of: 1. Palaeography: ancient handwriting is studied very carefully to establish the changes in style which occurred over the years; 2. Pottery: similarly, the pots used for storing the Dead Sea Scrolls reveal changes in the shape of the pots and the markings on the outsides of them over the years; 3. Linen: the linen used for wrapping around the scrolls can be carbon-dated. The linen, being made from organic material, starts to decrease in radioactivity from the time it is cut. This gives a guide date as to when the linen was made and the extant date of the manuscript; 4. Numismatics: the coins found in the caves can be dated from 140 BCE to 70 CE. Items 2, 3, and 4 are considered to be merely corroborative evidence; the principal evidence comes from 1, i.e., palaeography.

In spite of some differences in the grammatical forms and spellings, Dr. Burrows, in his book (see bibliography) has identified 13 references in which the Qumran text of Isaiah differs from the Masoretic text, which was adopted as the Received Text used by the translators of the King James Version (KJV). They are Isaiah 3:24, 14:4, 14:30, 15:9, 21:8, 23:2, 33:8, 45:2, 45:8, 49:24, 51:19, 56:12, and 60:19. These references were considered by the Committee of the Revised Standard Version in consideration of the new revision. Each verse was considered to see whether the Qumran text should be used in place of the Masoretic text. It was decided by a majority vote which reading to adopt. Of the 13 variants, 8 that were adopted were also supported by Greek, Aramaic, Syriac or Latin ancient translations. The remaining 5 variants were supported only by the Qumran text. All 13 are here detailed so that the reader may judge how significant the differences are, as follows: 1. In Isaiah 14:4, the Received Text ends with, "how has the oppressor ceased! The golden city ceased," whereas the Qumran text has "how the oppressor has ceased, the insolent fury ceased," which the ancient translations support to some degree. 2. In Isaiah 14:30, the Received Text has the words "he will slay," whereas the Qumran text ends the verse with the words "I will slay." 3. In Isaiah 15:9, the Received Text refers to a city named Dimon. This city is not known. Instead, the Qumran text and

23

the Latin translation give the name as Dibon, which is well known. 4. In Isaiah 29:24, the Received Text has the words "the captives of a righteous man", while the Qumran text, with the support of the Syriac and Latin translations, has "the captives of a tyrant". 5. In Isaiah 45:2, "rough places" in the Received Text is replaced by "the mountains." 6. In Isaiah 51:19, the Received Text ends with the words "how may I comfort you?" whereas the Qumran text, supported by ancient translations, ends with the words "who will comfort you?" 7. In Isaiah 56:12, instead of "let me get wine" in the Received Text, the Qumran has "let us get wine." 8. In Isaiah 60:19, the Received Text ends the verse with the words "light to you", whereas the Qumran text, supported by the ancient translations, includes the words "by night" after "light to you."

In the other 5 of the 13 changes made in the RSV, the only supporting evidence has come from the Qumran text. 1. In Isaiah 3:24, the Received Text ends the verse with the words "instead of beauty." The Qumran text completes the verse by adding "shame" at the end of the verse. 2. In Isaiah 21:8, the Received Text has the words "and he cried, a lion" or "as a lion." The Qumran has "he who saw." The Received Text has a different wording because, in Hebrew, the sounds are not dissimilar and the text could have been copied by dictation. A scriptorium has been discovered at the Qumran complex. Part of the scribes' daily routine was

24

to make copies to replace worn out scrolls. 3. In Isaiah 23:2, in the Received Text the Hebrew wording for "they replenished you" which sounds similar to that for "your messengers," which is the reading of the Qumran text. 4. In Isaiah 33:8, the Received Text has the Hebrew wording for "cities" which once again is similar sounding to that for "witnesses," the wording of the Qumran text. 5. In Isaiah 45:8, the Received Text wording of "that they may bring forth salvation" should be replaced by "that salvation may sprout forth" from the Qumran text.

In spite of there being just 13 verses in the 66 chapters of Isaiah with differences between the Received Text and the Qumran text, this exercise shows how good a job the Masoretes had done in copying the text over a period of 1,000 years. Indeed, as Dr. Burrows points out, the Qumran text readings are not always demonstrably superior to the Masoretic text. In his view, even some of the 8 changes should not have been made. Considering all 13 changes, is there any change that substantially alters the sense or meaning of a verse? There is no evidence of this in this large book of Isaiah. The Hebrew University copy of the Isaiah scroll shows even closer agreement with the Masoretic Text. Dr. Burrows has similarly analysed the differences between the Masoretic Text and the text of the Dead Sea Scrolls, in the Book of Habakkuk. In agreement with Elligier, after a painstaking comparison between the Masoretic Text and the Dead Sea Scrolls, the conclusion of both scholars upholds the close agreement of the two texts. God has given us His Word and safeguarded it to those of us who revere the Scriptures, so that by studying them we may become wise unto salvation in Christ our Lord.

4. The English Bible

"Speak Lord, for your servant is listening. ... The Lord ... revealed himself to Samuel through his Word." (1 Samuel 3:9, 19)

Key to the process of having a Bible today that we can each read in our mother tongue is the skill of translation, the human cost and the hand of God. When we consider these facts, it causes our hearts to praise Him that He has engineered circumstances over thousands of years, so that today so many of us have a copy of His word and this can enable us to grow in love and knowledge of our Lord Jesus Christ. The translator has the twofold problem of rightly understanding a language and culture that existed thousands of years ago, and rightly render this into another language and culture. Clearly, he or she needs to be skilled in Hebrew, Aramaic, and Greek as well as the language into which the translation is to be made.

Amongst those who stand out in their devotion to the discovery and publication of Biblical MSS is Constantine Tischendorf. He continued to make repeated journeys to libraries, churches and monasteries seeking MSS, as far as the Saint Catherine monastery on Mount Sinai. Here he discovered 43 leaves of MSS, which were about to be burned and were in fact from Old Testament books of the Septuagint. He was allowed to take these sheets away and later realised this was no mean find, since they were written 100 years earlier than the previously known MSS of the Septuagint. An important and valuable feature of his work was that he published many editions of the Septuagint and the Greek New Testament incorporating his latest finds. He did this by developing a critical apparatus in which he identified the MSS that supported the variants from the Received Text. He returned 9 years later to the monastery and then a further 6 years later until on the last evening he remarked to the steward that he had brought a copy of the Septuagint he had recently produced. To his utter amazement, the steward said that he also had a copy of the Septuagint and he took down from a shelf a bundle of MSS leaves, 199 more of the Old Testament and the complete New Testament. Tischendorf rapidly set about publishing both MSS, so that both were available to the public by 1922. As a result of his labours, scholars now had available more than 8 editions of the Greek New Testament besides Codex Sinaticus and an improved, reliable copy of Codex Vaticanus which had so far remained inaccessible in the library of the Vatican.

There are accounts of Christianity coming to Britain, early in the 4th century, and amongst the many names in this connection are those of Augustine, Birinus, and Aidan. By the middle of the 7th century most of Britain had been given the message of Christ. The first translator of the Bible in Great Britain was Aldhelm, Bishop of Sherborne, having translated the Psalms. Bede and Wycliffe followed him, amongst others. Hitherto the official Bible was in Latin, whereas the common people had not been taught Latin. God was putting it now into the hearts of more people that they needed to read the Bible for themselves. William Tyndale, a graduate of Oxford and lecturer at Cambridge, caught the vision to which he devoted his whole life. This was, that the boy who operated the plough would become as knowledgeable in the Scriptures as the clergy who could read the Scriptures in Latin. He set about this undertaking by going back to the Greek to improve the translation which had previously been made from the Latin translations. His NT was completed in 1524, and printing started in 1525, but because his translation relied heavily on the Greek, changes in wording were resented by the Clergy and the State, whereas the public were eager to have an English Bible. He now started work on the OT, working from the Hebrew text and completed the Pentateuch by 1530. He then worked on the books from Joshua to Esther before his martyrdom because of his consuming desire to make the Word of God accessible to the average person. The value of his work was recognised after his martyrdom by other translators and incorporated into their translations. This was in the Bible of Coverdale (1535), Matthew's Bible (1537), the

Great Bible (1539) and the Geneva Bible (1560). The blood of this faithful servant of God was not shed in vain; his work carried on and bore fruit in the labours of subsequent translators.

With the accession of King James I, the need was felt for a new translation and this was to be carried out by the universities but to be approved by the bishops of the Church and ultimately by the King himself. In all there were 48 revisers, divided into six groups with two at Westminster, two at Oxford and two at Cambridge. No marginal notes were to be attached, but necessary explanations of Hebrew or Greek were allowed. Each group passed its work to the next group, until each group had seen all the books of the Bible. A general meeting of all the group leaders together with learned men who were invited enabled differences to be sorted out so that four years later in 1611 it was completed. This Authorised Version reigned supreme for nearly 300 years, but in the meantime new Greek and Hebrew MSS, together with translations in other languages, were uncovered. Also, since the Authorised Version (AV) was produced, scholars were continuing their studies with the new MSS that had been found and it soon became evident that the Received Text that was used for the AV was not entirely adequate. A new revision was called for and this was known as the Revised Version, started in 1870, and with considerable progress in textual studies, work was started on a new

Received Text. Two groups were formed in the UK and two in America, to whom all the alterations were sent. The alterations requested by the American groups were carefully considered, and if they were not adopted they were listed in an appendix. The completed work was published in 1885 with any changes to be made by majority votes and based on accuracy. The Revised Version was then followed by the American Standard Version in 1901 with the readings preferred by the American members. Several English translations followed which sought to take advantage of the Dead Sea Scrolls and other ancient MSS that were discovered. The Revised Standard Version was published in 1952 and this was followed by the New English Bible in 1970 with the translators being chosen from a team of international scholars who were charged with obtaining accuracy and natural, clear English. This was followed by the New International Version (NIV) in 1978, also using international, interdenominational scholars, all motivated by the desire to produce an accurate and clear version of the Word of God. Yet another translation, known as the English Standard Version (ESV) was published in 2011 with the help of a team of more than 100 international and interdenominational scholars and advisors. The underlying Hebrew text is the Masoretic text for the OT and the Novum Testamentum Graece (27th edition) for the NT, together with alternative renderings from the

Dead Sea Scrolls, the Septuagint, the Samaritan Pentateuch, and other translations. The ESV is an essentially literal translation and has the useful practice of using the same English word for recurring Hebrew or Greek words wherever possible, thereby facilitating academic study as well as clarity of expression. For all the translations referred to here, the reader will find more detail and the underlying philosophy of each translation in their prefaces and introductions.

Our Lord Jesus while on the earth read from, referred to and endorsed the OT Scriptures in the text as we have it today. Direct references to individual verses are made in Matthew 12:3–5, 12:39 42, 19:4–5, 21:16, 22:37, 22:41–45, Luke 4:21 and John 5:39, amongst others. He also frequently mentioned OT characters, David, Solomon, Abraham, Moses, Noah, Lot and his wife, Elijah, and the widow of Zarephath, Daniel, Abiathar, Isaac, Jacob, Naaman and the Queen of Sheba. He referred also to place names such as Sodom, Gomorrah, Tyre, Sidon and Nineveh. Not only did He refer to the texts, persons and places mentioned but He also based much of His teaching on the subjects of divorce and marriage, the Sabbath and His claim to be the Son of God. On the subject of marriage, He went straight back to the Book of Genesis, stating that in the beginning "the Creator made them male and female …. Therefore what God has joined together, let man not separate" (Matthew 19:5–6). On the subject of keeping the

Sabbath, Jesus' words again went straight back to the Scriptures: "Have you never read what David did when he and his companions were hungry and in need? In the days of Abiathar, the high priest, he entered the house of God" (Mark 2:25–6). To these examples can be added the definitive words of Jesus, "Man does not live on bread alone, but on every word that comes from the mouth of God" (Matthew 4:4). When the Jews vehemently opposed His claim to be the Son of God (John 10:33), Jesus once again appealed to the authority of Scripture with the words, "The Scriptures cannot be broken" (John 10:35). He repeatedly appealed to the Jews, saying, "These are the Scriptures that testify about me, yet you refuse to come to me to have life" (John 5:39–40). In the account of the rich man and Lazarus in Luke 16:19–31, Jesus finished with the telling words, "If they do not listen to Moses and the prophets they will not be convinced even if someone rises from the dead." How true those words of Jesus are, as we live in the days after his resurrection! It should be clearly plain to see the stamp of authority and truth that Jesus gave to the OT Scriptures. They have the power to shape and control our thinking and living.

There are numerous quotations and prophecies from the OT in the NT, thereby relating them both textually and in fulfilment. The New Covenant, established in the NT, is the fulfilment of the Old Covenant because it completes in Christ the work started in the OT. This knits the OT and NT together, since the OT has the full approval and accreditation of our Lord Jesus Christ, and also because the NT uses and relies on numerous quotations from the OT in fulfilled prophecy and support. Let us praise God that His hand has overruled in all circumstances and that evil men have been prevented from corrupting Scripture so that we have in our hands today an accurate copy of **The Word of God** to enable us to grow in our most holy faith. Even though we have this significant body of corroborative evidence to strengthen our faith, let it always be true that "we live by faith, not by sight" (2 Corinthians 5:7) because Jesus has said, "Blessed are those who have not seen and yet have believed." John 20:29.

5. The Word of God in Your Hand

And so we come to the Bible that you and I can hold in our hands today, translated into our own language with painstaking care from the original texts. It is a reliable and accurate account of the Word of God. God has preserved it throughout history, that today we might read it, and believe. The evidence for the NT is so strong in history, archaeology and the MSS, and since the NT totally reinforces and authenticates the OT how can one reasonably question the truth of our Bible today?

"These are written that you may believe that Jesus is the Messiah, the Son of God, and that by believing you may have life in his name." (John 20:31)

Bibliography and References

Those who have access to the internet may see sample images of the MSS of the OT and NT at the following websites:-

www.dss.collections.imj.org.il/isaiah;

www.bl.uk/onlinegallery/sacredtexts/codexalex_lg.html

www.imagesonline.bl.uk/, search for "Sinaiticus".

Bruce, F. F. 1950. The Books and the Parchments. Revell, 1963 ed.

Bruce, F. F. 1966. Second Thoughts on the Dead Sea Scrolls. Paternoster Press.

Burrows, M. 1956. The Dead Sea Scrolls. Secker and Warburg.

Gaebelein, F. E. 1979. The Expositors Bible Commentary. Vol. 1. Zondervan, 1979.

James, M. R. 1924. The Apocryphal New Testament. Oxford University Press.

Kenyon, F. G. 1936. The Story of the Bible: A Popular Account of How it Came to Us. London: J. Murray, 2nd ed. With supplementary material by F. F. Bruce. 1964 ed.

Kenyon, F. G. 1958. Our Bible and the Ancient Manuscripts. Forgotten Books. 2015 ed. www.archive.org/details/ourbibleandanci00kenygoog.

New Bible Dictionary. 1982. eds. A. R. Millard, J. I. Packer, and D. J. Wiseman. IVP, 2nd ed.